Within the pages of T
Investing for Women
beyond myths and theo
experience. The lessons she teacnes and the systems she shares will save many thousands of hours of effort in learning things the hard way. It's always great when someone who has been to the mountaintop is willing to show us the way.

Jim Stovall, best-selling author of *The Ultimate Gift*

Joanne Mendoza keeps it real as she guides the reader through a proven method of investing. Methods that are current, smart, and clear. Methods that Joanne uses daily in her real estate practice. The Power of Real Estate Investing for Women *is thoughtful and strategic with wealth building as the goal.* **A MUST READ***!*

Gretchen Pearson
President CEO
Berkshire Hathaway HomeServices
Drysdale Properties

Joanne's book will help you overcome limiting beliefs and get started on the path of successful real estate investing.

John Jay Rice, author of *All That Was Revealed: What the Shaman Taught Me*

The **POWER** of
Real Estate Investing for
WOMEN

STEP-BY-STEP GUIDE
TO INVESTING, HOLDING,
BUYING AND SELLING
REAL ESTATE

JOANNE MENDOZA CACANINDIN

OnFire Books
Helping world changers share their story

Clovercroft Publishing

Published by Clovercroft Publishing, Franklin, Tennessee

Edited by OnFire Books

Cover designed, and interior designed
by Adept Content Solutions

Printed in the United States of America

ISBN: 978-1-950892-73-0

Contents

So many people will tell you "no," and you need to find something you believe in so hard that you just smile and tell them "watch me." Learn to take rejection as motivation to prove people wrong. Be unstoppable. Refuse to give up, no matter what. It's the best skill you can ever learn.

Charlotte Eriksson

Introduction

*Hope lies in dreams, in imagination, and in the courage
of those who dare to make dreams into reality.*

Jonas Salk

*What is your dream? Whatever it is, you can do it,
if you take action every day.*

I am a realtor and a real estate investor.

So why would I want to write a book?

The answer is simple. I believe we are here to share a part of ourselves, do good in the world, and to help others succeed in whatever their goals may be. Writing a book was one of my dreams as a way to capture what I've learned and pass that wisdom on, but I never knew it would be a reality.

After years of dedicating the majority of my waking hours to the real estate and investment industry, learning all its facts and fictions, its ins and outs, that's when I knew it was time to write my book.

Let me begin by confessing that I'm not a writer. I've never written anything that's been published: no articles, newsletters, or anything of the kind. I have a message that

I think is valuable to women from all walks of life (also to the men with whom my message resonates). I would like to impart my knowledge, my perspective, and years of experience as a real estate investor and broker so anyone can learn from my mistakes and share in my achievements.

I've been through many trials and tribulations in this business—from moments of panic to finally having a system in place—and I've finally reached the point where it's time to "pay it forward," focusing on scaling up my business and helping others do what I've done. I woke up one day and had this burning desire to share what I know about investing in real estate in the hope it will ignite women who are on the fence, who have thought about investing but don't know where to begin, or who are already investing but are feeling stuck. My hope is that the messages in these pages will bring value and that it will be as easy to understand as it is relatable. I would like to think of my approach like a recipe, with clear and concise ingredients to follow.

Life wasn't always easy or simple for me. I am an immigrant from the Philippines. I came to the United States when I was around six or seven years old. There were six of us at the time: my parents; my older sister, Jeana; and twin sisters, Gaye and Gail. Our only possessions were in suitcases filled with meager clothes. We didn't have much else. We stayed with relatives in Daly City, California, crammed into a 10 × 10 room. From what I recall, my older sister and I shared a small bed while the twins slept with my parents.

Luckily, after a couple of years, my dad was able to save up enough money to move us to a two-bedroom apartment in Mountain View, California. I was excited. I think we were all happy to have our own place with lots of room and a swimming pool in the complex—which turned out to be a bad idea because one of the twins had a near-death drowning accident.

Our third move was a few cities south, to San Jose, California. It was a three-bedroom house that we loved, a ranch-style home with plenty of room for us. My older sister and I shared a room while the twins had theirs. There was enough space in the backyard for us to run around in, and we even had a few animals and a nice garden. Our school was within walking distance. Our neighbors were also our schoolmates, which made this home even more special. It was in a good neighborhood. I thought this house would be our very own home at last.

Unfortunately, my dad's friend, who was supposed to have helped him purchase the house, screwed him over with the deed and money, therefore crushing our dreams to millions of little pieces! We were all devastated.

My dad decided that he needed to make money fast, so he left for Saudi Arabia to work there for a few years while we stayed with my mom to care for our siblings. By this time, a new member of our family, Irish, joined us. My mom also learned how to drive so she could take us places and run errands. Driving was something that petrified my mom, and it did not help that we had a big blue Dodge van that she felt was as unwieldy as a large RV every time she drove it on the streets of San Jose. I remembered how scared she was, demanding my older sister and I to be her other set of eyes, to look right or left as she turned or changed lanes. But she was determined and, soon after, conquered the world of driving.

After several years of saving, we moved out of San Jose to a new development in the East Bay, to a little town called West Pittsburg. It was desolate and eerie as we were one of the few families to move in the community known as Lynbrook.

I come from a large family with six sisters, a half-brother, and an extended family with whom we are very close. I have nieces and nephews that I hope will one day read my book and grasp something important from the pages and make a name for themselves in the real estate world. I hope to make a difference in their lives.

I am not much different from you. I am just like anyone else who chose to set goals, create a vision, and follow a dream. I believe that the secret of receiving is in being able to give. I hope that my story will encourage and inspire you.

What is your vision? What are your goals? What are your dreams? Where do you want to be in five years from now? How about in twenty years? I hope to inspire you to live your life, no matter where you are or what profession you are in.

We all have limiting beliefs—about income, family, race, or sexuality. We must all learn to conquer those self-imposed limitations and build new empowering ones about our abilities to succeed in whatever we choose to do. It's not about the limiting beliefs themselves; it's about what you choose to do with them. Trust me—you can be whatever you want to be if you make the decision not to let your limitations hold you back.

This book consists of lessons. I hope to challenge your beliefs and ask you questions that will inspire you to think deeply. At the end of each lesson are three blank pages for you to write your key takeaways, questions, or ideas. I encourage you to spend some time after reading each lesson, jotting down whatever the lesson brings to mind. It is said that thoughts and goals put on paper will come to fruition faster than keeping them in your mind. That's why there are so many classes in goal writing. It is my hope that this book will serve as a reference for you for years to come.

Let the learning begin. I learned real estate investing. *You can too!*

Investing Isn't Just for Men

We must believe that we are gifted for something, and
that this thing, at whatever cost, must be attained.

Marie Curie

Let's face it. Many of the books on success today are written by men. Every time I search online, looking for an investment book, I notice that most of these books are not written by female authors. Believe me, I have read lots of them! Although I resonate with and have learned greatly from men and their passion to serve and do well in real estate, I would love to see something written by a woman, for women. Specifically, I'd like to see a real estate investment book written for women. That is why I am writing this book.

I'm not negatively targeting males, but I think it's important that women ought to contribute as well. I find it comforting to know that in some small way, I may be paving the way toward that goal by sharing real estate investing from a woman's perspective. Of course, I hope men will enjoy this book as well by reading the lessons I present here from a woman's point of view.

The gender gap in real estate investment is factual, and it is damaging to women's financial health. According to "Why More Women Should Invest in Real Estate" in the February 2019 edition of *Forbes* magazine, there are many women who are real estate agents, but not nearly as many who are real estate investors. The article states, "According to a 2018 study by Fidelity Investments, only 29 percent of women see themselves as investors, and less than one in four women are comfortable with their knowledge of investing."[1]

The gender gap in real estate investment is factual, and it is damaging to women's financial health.

Wow! Why are so many women uncomfortable with their knowledge of investing? Is it because we are too busy taking care of children and trusting our men to do the financial heavy lifting? Or is it because real estate investing is intimidating to us and our limiting beliefs keep us from getting the financial education we need? Or is it a little of both?

If you are a woman who has never invested in real estate, what is your reason for not investing? Write it down on the pages provided at the end of this lesson.

We women need to be more practical in empowering ourselves in our financial lives. Why? Because, on average, women tend to live longer than men. Shouldn't we be taught to invest wisely so that we can live comfortably as we age? Many women keep the majority of their money in savings accounts. That's not a bad thing, but perhaps we are missing an opportunity to build wealth and security for ourselves when we don't educate ourselves about investment opportunities. We are missing opportunities for potential double-digit returns and big tax advantages. We are missing opportunities for that dream family vacation, the ability to send our kids to the best universities and, most importantly, the opportunity to create passive residual income (i.e., income generated when we are not working).

It is my hope that this book will also serve empowered young women who want to start building their future by doing something different. There are many ways to build wealth today. If you're open to the possibilities, the wealth-building opportunities are truly endless. I believe the younger generation can begin paving their way into the real estate investing world because I find them to be the most energetic and eager risk-takers. With the proper guidance, they can be comforted in knowing there is a recipe that is easy to follow. It is no longer necessary for women to follow the conventional paths of our mothers and grandmothers—the ideas for wealth building that my parents' generation instilled in the minds of their seven children. What kinds of financial strategies were you taught? Take a minute to write them down.

Chances are, if you are like most women, you were taught to go to school, earn a degree, graduate, get a stable job, get married, have kids, buy a house, and stay in your job with your two weeks of vacation as long as possible, all while saving money in your 401(k) for your retirement and trying to juggle your life to fit around your job. That is, if you didn't get laid off or had to leave your job to take care of children or elderly parents. If you managed to do all of these things, then maybe, if you are lucky, after you've retired and if you're still healthy, you can enjoy the fruits of your retirement after slaving away in an office for nearly an entire lifetime.

That's the conventional way of thinking, and that was what my parents' generation found security in doing, but the same isn't true today. Most of the dependable companies where one could enjoy job security for forty years have come and gone, and it's hard to keep a steady job because we live in a world where things change at warp speed. We are living in a technological world where a product could be deemed obsolete in a matter of months! That phone, for example—your new iPhone, Samsung, or Google device that you own today—could be replaced by a newer version the week after. The underlying assumption in the messages that many of us received from our parents is that we should all follow the same linear path and that there is no other way to achieve wealth. The assumption is that only *after* we retire will we be free to explore the world, spend time with friends and family, or learn a new skill just for the fun of it. I'm here to tell you that there is "no one-size-fits-all" approach to wealth building, and I can tell you from experience that you do not have to wait until you are a seasoned and retired individual to enjoy financial freedom.

So what does financial freedom mean to you? Write it down.

Financial freedom means that you have enough money coming in that you no longer need to trade your hours for your paycheck. Of course, there are many combinations of ways that people can achieve financial freedom, and they all require some effort up front. In today's ever-changing world, the good news is that real estate investing hasn't changed much over the years. The tactics may be different today, but the logistics, fundamentals, and products haven't changed. It's simple, but not easy. You buy a piece of real estate and what do you do with it? Hold it for cash-flow? Fix and flip, wholesale, or live in it?

Financial freedom means that you have enough money coming in that you no longer need to trade your hours for your paycheck.

Most Americans invest in one piece of real estate and live in it for the rest of their lives. But it is possible to build wealth in ways other than buying one house to live in. I'll cover each subtopic in the later chapters.

Women in the Generation X and Baby Boomer generations will benefit from this book just as much as women in the younger generation. By learning the basics and following recommendations, you too can begin taking your first steps toward real estate investing. No matter your age, this book will serve you as you learn from the experiences of successful women who share their step-by-step solutions in an easy-to-understand guide. Whether you are a beginner or an expert, there's something for everyone within these pages. It doesn't matter where you come from, your background, the color of your skin, or how old you are. What matters is where you want to go. Where *do* you want to go? Wherever it is, know that it's all in your hands and that it's possible. I can guide you through the basics, but you will have to do the work. You will be required to look at your limiting beliefs through new eyes and become very clear about your focus and action plans. You will need to manage your state of mind and try new things, even when you are feeling fearful. You will need to develop the habits of a successful investor. These habits will carry through to so many other areas in your life. You will become more confident, bold, and analytical.

Sound overwhelming? It doesn't have to be. Take it slowly. Read this book. Talk it over with someone you trust. Spend time absorbing the lessons until you know them like the back of your hand.

Let this be your guidebook. It's like you are traveling to a foreign country where you don't know anything, but you've got this book as a great guide. As you read and follow the instructions, you begin to understand the best sights to see and the best places to eat. Once you get these basics down, you can pick and choose which direction you want to take.

Just as everyone does not take the same route when they visit a new place, not everyone follows the same path when learning real estate investing. Investing is kind of like trying a direction, and if it feels good to you, you go with it. If it doesn't feel right, then you try a different direction or approach. The important point here is that you're taking action. One can read a plethora of books and never take action, but for those who do, a great reward awaits.

More women need to start making financial wellness a top priority. We need to address not only the pay gap that we know exists between men and women in the United States, but we must also address the knowledge gap as it pertains to financial literacy.

You will be required to look at your limiting beliefs through new eyes and become very clear about your focus and action plans.

So where should you start? Just as you would any new undertaking—with baby steps. Learn to walk before you expect to run. Tell others that you are learning about real estate investing and engage in exchanges of ideas. You might be surprised at how others can support you and contribute to your knowledge, or you may find that they are just getting their feet wet too!

If you are already investing, whether you are successful or having challenges, this book shares ideas which may bring a new light or direction, enhancements, and systems to push you forward and give new life to your real estate investing.

You don't have to wait for your retirement; if you have the desire, drive, and determination, combined with a hunger for financial freedom, this book is for you. In fact, for anyone who wants a better future, to create a new standard, to revise the conventional lifestyle, or to live life on your own terms, this book is for you.

_____

_____

_____

_____

_____

_____

_____

_____

_____

_____

_____

_____

_____

_____

_____

_____

_____

_____

_____

_____

_____

_____

_____

_____

_____

_____

_____

_____

_____

_____

_____

_____

_____

_____

_____

_____

_____

_____

_____

_____

_____

_____

_____

_____

_____

_____

_____

_____

_____

_____

_____

_____

_____

_____

_____

_____

Only 25 percent of investment purchase decisions are made by women. Is that acceptable to you? It is not acceptable to me, because I know we can do better than that.

Why Women (Or Anyone) Should Invest in Real Estate

Being a strong woman is very important to me. But doing it all on my own is not.

Reba McEntire

We know that in the business world, women are typically paid less than men. And it amazes me that even now, we are still fighting that battle. There is no simple reason for this disparity between men and women, and thus, no simple solution to this disparity.

Women have made great strides in their claims for equality in workplace leadership, but we still have a long way to go. Males in business leadership positions may not always be aware of the many obstacles women face. As women strive to fit in a male-dominated business world, they often feel they have to be "on guard" with men in order to avoid misunderstandings in the workplace. This can add a lot of stress to women leaders' positions.

It's always surprising to me when I hit the wall of prejudice pertaining to the way people perceive women in business versus men. Often, in this industry, men are seen as the investors, and because women are so rare in this industry, they're often overlooked. Here's the irony.

According to a November 2018 article on the Bigger Pockets' website (a site dedicated to creating wealth through real estate), women make or influence 91 percent of the home-buying decisions in this country. That's a whopping nine out of ten property purchase decisions that are made by women![1]

So where's the problem?

According to the article, if you add the word *investment* in front of the word *property*, suddenly those numbers drop to 2.5 out of 10 decisions that are being made by women.[2] That means only 25 percent of investment purchase decisions are made by women. Is that acceptable to you? It is not acceptable to me, because I know we can do better than that.

The author of this article describes how men and women consume information about investing differently and compared the differences between men and women investment groups. What's an investment group? These groups (or clubs, as they are sometimes called) meet locally on a regular basis. They can provide networking and learning

---

[1] Erin Spradlin, "Women Influence 91% of Homebuying Purchases. So Why Aren't More Investing?" BiggerPockets (blog), Nov. 27, 2019, https://www.biggerpockets.com/blog/women-home-buying-purchases.

[2] Ibid.

opportunities for both beginners and experienced investors. They can help you learn about reputable contractors, brokers, realtors, lawyers, and accountants. Not all real estate investing groups are reputable or have your best interests in mind. It is important to know what you're getting into should you choose to get involved.

The author of the Bigger Pockets article argues that men tend to be comfortable with a higher level of risk than women.[3] She believes that there is a stronger sense of bravado, loudness, and quickness to act in groups where men are in the majority.[4] In many ways, she says, women's groups are the same as their male counterparts with regard to the sharing of resources and information.[5] However, she advocates that groups designed for women should be smaller, quieter, and allow plenty of time for a speaker to present information while giving everyone time to ask any and all questions.[6] She believes that rather than complaining about the differences between how men and women approach investing, we should be addressing how to make women feel more comfortable in a male-dominated space.[7]

All of this is great information about the gender disparity in real estate investing, but it's just numbers. At some point,

[3] Ibid.

[4] Spradlin, "Women Influence 91% of Homebuying Purchases," https://www.biggerpockets.com/blog/women-home-buying-purchases.

[5] Ibid.

[6] Ibid.

[7] Ibid.

we have to not focus so much on the disparity (after all, life isn't fair!) and just become more resilient and smarter.

When I started on this journey, I really didn't know where to begin or go for information. We were not on the internet when I got my first job in the mortgage industry, circa 1990. I was doing temporary work for Sears Mortgage back then, and because of my work ethic and hard-working mentality, they hired me on as a full-time data processor. That meant I input new loans (both refinance and purchase) into a software system. I always knew I wanted more, and I had the hunger to excel within the company. I was gradually but

We should be addressing how to make women feel more comfortable in a male dominated space.

consistently climbing the ladder to this career, and I was very happy and proud of myself. All the while, at that point in my life and career, the idea of being self-employed never crossed my mind. As a woman in her mid-40s, I guess you could say I was a bit late to the game of real estate investing, even though I had worked in it for decades. I've always considered myself an action-taker and a risk-taker, but business was not at top of my mind at the time. I can jump out of an airplane, free-fall 250 meters off a skyscraper, summit 14,508 feet up a mountain, and free-fall snowboard off a cliff. Those activities are easy risks for me, but when it came to money and wealth-building schemes, I felt limited to the resources around me, or perhaps I wasn't open to the possibilities yet and let others do the investing for me. They say the teacher will appear when the student is ready. Perhaps I wasn't ready then. I didn't have a mentor, a coach, nor even knew of anyone in the field of real estate investing, so I had no one to emulate or ask for guidance.

Until one day, in January 2015, when I decided to take action. This was not a quick step, although in hindsight, if I had read a book like this, I would've started sooner. Hearing of my relatives' investment endeavors out of state was the seed that grew in my mind and prompted me to take action. One comment I vividly recall hearing in 2013 was "Investing out-of-state is great. I just have my property manager handle the properties and every month, I get a check in the mail. It's great!" The only property they had owned prior to investing was the house they lived in. They encouraged me to watch a webinar and listen to a podcast (which I mention in a later chapter). This was pivotal for me. I guess you could say it ended up being my mentor and coach (indirectly speaking), inspiring me through other people's successes.

Since January 2015, I have not stopped. The momentum grows each year, and every time I look over my portfolio, I always ask myself, How can I accumulate more? How can I scale up? I then answer those questions by adding more and scaling up! As the saying goes, "Ask and ye shall receive."

Have you ever heard the expression "done is better than perfect"? It means that sometimes you just have to take a step and not worry if what you're doing is flawless. Napoleon Hill says if you don't know where to start, find a rock, throw it up in the air, and wherever it lands, that's where you begin.[8] I've noticed that women more than men tend to get caught up on analyzing things until they are perfect. If you've ever heard the phrase "analysis paralysis," then you know what I mean.

Here's the thing: You don't have to know everything to start. You are going to make mistakes, and that is okay. The truth is, making mistakes is part of the process, and this roadblock of failure or mistake is where you must recognize that it's part of the process. Push on and push forward because this decision is what will alter your course to curve either the path of success or the path of failure or mediocrity. You just have to take one baby step at a time. Slowly but surely. There are women investing today who are doing marvelous work. They started just like you and me, saying no to analysis paralysis and taking a step.

I recently met Holly Williams, from Woodstock, New York. She leaves me in awe. She went from zero to sixty properties in a matter of a few years. People usually start small, buying one property, like a condo, a townhouse, or a single-family home, to start. After they get the hang of it, they then start taking bigger steps toward duplexes, triplexes, or fourplexes. They might scale to even bigger apartment complexes.

But not Holly. She went from buying her first property in 1992, straight into investing in apartment complexes. These aren't your average 20 to 50 or even 100 units. She's taken monumental steps and scaled up in a matter of just a few years from 150 to now 350 units per complex where she manages hundreds of millions of dollars in her portfolio. Along with her partner, she currently owns nine complexes. She definitely had the right mind-set to scale at this level despite the challenges previously mentioned. She was determined and resilient. I know she had challenges, but she kept going. Great discipline and focus is key to scaling at this level. Now, I will be going into the subject of habits of a successful investor in another lesson. I share Holly's story here to show you all the possibilities that are potentially available. She really is the exception to the rule.

You can be like Holly or you can choose your own path. It really is up to you. The sky is the limit, if you will. There is no ceiling as to how high you can go. The key message here is

People usually start small, buying one property, like a condo, a townhouse, or a single-family home, to start.

to begin by taking action. Although I'm sure Holly can retire now and just lie on the beach and drink margaritas, I don't think it's what she's doing. She's enjoying this journey. Loving what you do isn't work; it's fun and exciting every day.

Your comfort zone is called a comfort zone for a reason. It's comfortable. It feels safe. It's tempting to stay there because it's what you know. I'm going to nudge you to take small steps outside of your comfort zone. There are many self-help books and articles out there to help you create strategies to challenge your comfort zone. Find a compelling reason to do something new. If you are thinking of getting started in real estate investing, why do you want to do it? Write down your reasons. If you are a seasoned investor, why did you start in the first place? Revisit your reasons. Have they changed?

Look back on other goals you have achieved in your life. How did you feel when you first started? Were you nervous? Did you make mistakes?

Self-talk is important. Tell yourself you are fearless. Did you know that your brain doesn't know the difference between reality and what you believe? If you tell yourself you are fearless, then soon your brain will believe it. Try

Find a compelling reason to do something new.

something new every day—something that makes you a little uncomfortable. Try doing it first thing in the morning—like taking a cold shower for one minute after your warm one, reading ten pages, or doing 100 jumping jacks. This way, you will feel empowered all day. The truth is that all the books and classes under the sun won't get you out of your comfort zone if *you* don't take that one baby step to do something differently.

Women, I urge you to get out of your comfort zone. I know you have a lot on your plate, from juggling kids (for those mothers out there) to working, putting food on the table, shopping, doing laundry, cleaning house, putting on make-up, getting your nails done, and figuring out what outfit to wear for the day. We have so much to think about—trust me, I know—but adding on this one significant practice could mean the freedom you've been aching to have.

Imagine being able to buy what you want, go where you want, to upgrade the life you have and be where you were meant to be, and to pay someone else to do the tedious work for you, like cleaning your house or houses or running your errands. If you think about it, most women can do all of these things blindfolded, but we didn't get good at them in one day. It took time, lots of practice, and watching others perform these duties day after day. That's what investing in real estate is like; you won't be good at it at first, but through reading and watching, you'll learn enough to take the first step forward to take action.

It's time to take action. What are you waiting for? You are *not* alone!

_____

_____

_____

_____

_____

_____

_____

_____

_____

_____

_____

_____

_____

_____

_____

_____

_____

_____

_____

_____

_____

_____

_____

_____

_____

_____

_____

_____

_____

_____

_____

_____

_____

_____

_____

_____

_____

_____

Understanding Financing and Leveraging
Why Is Borrowing Better Than Cash?

Every financial worry you want to banish and financial dream you want to achieve comes from taking tiny steps today that put you on a path toward your goals.

Suze Orman

To begin the real estate investing platform, let's begin to understand the pertinence of leverage. What does it mean to leverage? Look at the word. It has the word *lever* in it. Think of high school science and learning about levers and fulcrums. A lever can be used to help you move something that you may not be able to move on your own. In terms of real estate investing, leveraging is the idea of using borrowed capital or debt to increase your potential for a higher return on your investment.

I didn't understand this concept or its benefits early on in my career in the lending industry, so I had to learn the hard way. Climbing the ladder within the mortgage/lending industry proved to be an advantage for me. After learning each position from data entry to being a supervisor and traveling nationally to set up and arrange start-ups of other branches to being a doc drawer, senior funder, senior loan processor, senior underwriter, and account executive, I learned what goes in the life of a loan from every possible perspective.

When the market got hot in 2001–2006, I began leveraging by borrowing. I also took it a step further and put mortgages in my name on behalf of my siblings. Boy, what a mistake that was because when the market crashed, guess who got the worst of it? Guess who got stuck holding the mortgages? That's right, me. Holding six mortgage loans in my name created a bad situation, as when our industry imploded, so did my credit score—something I had been so proud of building for years.

My sisters lost their jobs and couldn't make payments, so everything came crashing down. Renting those properties never even crossed my mind. In hindsight, I would have planned much better if I knew then what I know now. I hope you will learn from my mistakes.

Leverage is about using other people's money. Here are some examples of places where you can leverage those funds. You can borrow through conventional lenders like Chase, Bank of America, or Wells Fargo, who will lend based on good credit FICO scores with as little as a 3 percent down payment. Also consider a retail lending institution like Summit Funding or Quicken Loans, which have the flexibility of offering other nonconventional loan programs that can either be kept in-house or sold to a secondary wholesale market. Credit unions can also provide home loans. They tend to be more conservative but often offer their members the lowest rate.

A mortgage broker (like Omni Funding, Mason McDuffie, RPM, or American Pacific Mortgage) is an intermediary (a.k.a., a loan officer) who shops around to find you the best rates through their pool of approved secondary loan purchasers like Flagstar, Chase, Bank of America, and so forth. using FNMA, Freddie Mac, and Ginnie Mae guidelines to sell to them immediately after you close. There are also hard-money lenders who will offer a much higher interest rate with fees and points and lower loan to value (LTV): This means you would have to bring in more money in order to close.

Leverage is about using other people's money.

This option is more for those who do not have good credit or want a quicker close and have a good chunk of money as down payment. They also look at the property more closely, as collateral is more important than scores. They lend on short-term loan programs, meaning they will only finance that property for up to five years, which can be amortized over twenty or thirty years, but with a balloon payment at the end of five-year term. This is meant as a temporary loan holder because as your credit gets better, you can eventually refinance out of that hard money loan into a more traditional conventional loan and lower your interest rate.

Private money lenders are people like your grandparents, parents, aunts and uncles, siblings, relatives, friends, and anyone else who's willing to lend you money. There are less common sources such as crowdsourcing, crowdfunding, venture capitalists, and syndications where a group of people invest in other commodities or collaterals for the chance of increasing their net worth or on the basis that the product will go up in value and equity over time. These groups can lend money as well.

When you borrow money, using conventional or nonconforming loan in a traditional way, the lender will want to know that you can qualify for that loan and be creditworthy enough to be able to pay them back. This means a plethora of documents will be required from you at the onset. They'll begin by having you complete a loan application, then they'll pull your credit report based on your social security number. Once the report comes back and they're satisfied with the outcome, they'll request income documentation. That means if you work for a company, you'll provide your W2s, paystubs, and last two years of tax returns. If you're self-employed, you will be asked for 1099s, bank statements, and tax returns. Lenders will also ask for assets like statements from your bank accounts (or wherever the funds will come from) and will usually require extra for reserves (like statements from a 401k, Roth IRA, or retirement accounts). Be sure to provide them with all pages. The reason for this is that they're looking for any deposit that's out of the ordinary, like a large deposit or a huge deduction. If there is evidence shown of a large deposit, they'll ask for proof of this deposit or an explanation, and if the explanation is not reasonable, they may not let you use those funds and require you to provide proof of other assets.

Remember that the reason for providing these documents is so that the lender will be in a comfortable-enough position to know you'll pay them back. The general premise of all this document gathering is to determine whether you are capable of paying the lender back. People who have good FICO scores (680 or above) tend to pay their bills consistently and on time, thus making them the primary candidates for borrowing money.

Hard money and private lenders won't require as many documents, but they'll charge higher fees like points (also called origination fees). For example, on a 2 percent fee, if your loan amount is $500,000, this amount would be $10,000, and

> # The general premise of all this document gathering is to determine whether you are capable of paying the lender back.

rates are typically above 7 percent. As I explained previously, they'll require more money down, at least 30 percent. These are usually short-term loans, as minimal as six months to possibly five years. They're basing their comfort level on the collateral (the property), so if you end up not being able to pay them back and default on the loan, just like a traditional lender, they'll take back that collateral through a process called foreclosure and usually turn around and rent to tenants or sell to another buyer for a higher profit.

Federal Housing Authority (FHA) loans are loans backed by the government to ensure lenders that if the borrower defaults, the lender continues to receive their money. Although this is a great way to get started purchasing your first owner-occupied home, there are costs involved. This program is for owner occupied only and only requires a minimum down payment of 3.5 percent. For example, if you borrow $100,000, you're only required to put $3,500 down, which is great for those first-time buyers who don't have a lot of money saved. The lender will finance the remaining 96.5 percent LTV.

With the FHA program, the down payment can also be given to the borrower from a family member, such as parents, grandparents, aunts and uncles, and siblings. Technically, the money cannot come from friends, coworkers, or acquaintances, nor can it be borrowed. With FHA, one of the main costs involved is the payment of mortgage insurance (MI). Some lenders will collect up to 2.5 percent of MI fees up front, then charge a monthly MI payment (which is included in your mortgage payment). This is the portion that goes to the government as insurance in case the borrower has a problem paying their mortgage payment.

For someone starting out who wants to buy their first home and doesn't have a lot of money to put down, this program is a great option. A minimum FICO score of 580 is all that's necessary to qualify. The higher your FICO score, however, the more options you have with other lenders and more available loan programs out there. This can be coupled with using a DPA, (a.k.a., a Down-Payment Assistance program). But it is only for within your community or the area you purchase in that the government has allotted funds toward these home purchases. Not all buyers will qualify or fit in this box, but if everything works out right, you could end up getting back the 3.5 percent you put in as down payment and your earnest money deposit. Ask your local lender for details on these down-payment assistance programs before making a decision on which loan program to go with. But imagine buying a home and getting money back from it! I have seen it happen many times, so I know these programs are out there. Just look around and ask about them.

The Veterans Administration (VA) and United States Department of Agriculture (USDA) offer loan programs that offer 100 percent LTV financing. Isn't this great? For serving or having served our country, you reap the benefits of putting zero down. The USDA loans are also known as the USDA Rural Development Guaranteed Housing Loan Program. This is a mortgage loan program offered to rural property owners. With these programs, you have the option of putting money down if you choose, but it's not required. If you can qualify for this type of loan, up to 100 percent financing, take advantage of it. This and the DPA are great examples of leveraging at its best. You hardly have to put out any money from your pocket.

"House-hacking" is a term used quite often on real estate investing websites like Bigger Pockets (https://www.biggerpockets.com/). This website is a great resource for anything and everything related to real estate investing. They offer podcasts where they interview people at all levels of investing: How they got started and, how each baby step took them further and further in the real estate investing world.

House-hacking is someone else paying or helping to pay your owner-occupied mortgage. If you own a single-family home with three bedrooms, you can live in one of the bedrooms and rent out the other two. You collect room-rents and use that money toward paying down your mortgage. For example, with a three-bedroom home, if your mortgage payment is $1,600, you might rent the other two bedrooms for $600 each. That way only $400 of the mortgage comes out of your pocket. Better yet, if your renter pays enough to cover your monthly mortgage payment altogether, then you might live in your own home mortgage free. How great is that concept?

House-hacking works best when you own a duplex (or two-unit property) or an in-law unit (a separate building on your property, known today as ADU, or Accessory Dwelling Unit). You would rent out one unit while living in the other. I like this concept best because you still have your

House-hacking is someone else paying or helping to pay your owner-occupied mortgage.

privacy. Your tenant lives next door, and each month you are receiving rent, which helps pay down your mortgage balance. Sometimes the rent itself can cover your mortgage payment, allowing you to live payment-free. You can divert that money elsewhere toward another real estate deal. This is house-hacking at its best.

There are so many options of leveraging that when people say they can't wrap their heads around the concept, my answer to them is always, "Yes, you can." Usually people who believe they cannot do it are not educated on all the options available. It's not that they do not know or cannot do it, it's just that they do not have the right information.

I can say that the resources are out there. This book is one of them. Use it as your daily guide to understanding how leveraging works and can work for you. You must be willing to do a little research to educate yourself. The time it takes is worth it, and the valuable knowledge and information you'll gain to understand your options is even better. You can begin making the right decisions for you.

If you think of the time you spend on this as an action item toward your financial security and freedom, it's worth it. And once you begin to learn, it will all become easier and understandable.

Yes, it's intimidating at first. I've heard many women say "I'm not good at math." Well, that's a myth too.

Yes, some people are better at numbers than others, but it is a learned skill, and you can learn it too if you practice, practice, practice. If you don't understand the math involved, ask someone to explain it to you and go over it again and again until you feel confident. The internet is also a great resource, and places like YouTube—where you can watch someone explain this to you in the comfort of your own living room, over and over again, if necessary—are invaluable assets to your learning process.

Armed with the necessary knowledge, it's now time to take a deep breath—and take action. Step out of your comfort zone. What are your questions about the types of leveraging available to you? Write them down on the blank pages provided at the end of this lesson. Then make it your mission to get answers. It's okay to move slowly, but not moving at all is not going to get you the financial freedom you and your family deserve.

_____

_____

_____

_____

_____

_____

_____

_____

_____

_____

_____

_____

_____

_____

_____

_____

_____

_____

_____

_____

_____

_____

_____

_____

_____

_____

_____

_____

_____

_____

_____

_____

_____

_____

_____

_____

_____

_____

Build Wealth One Investment at a Time

Building wealth takes patience, discipline, and hard work.

clevergirlfinance.com

Defining the meaning of wealth to you is an important part of your deciding whether or not to take these baby steps to wealth building. What does the word *wealth* mean to you? Hint: Money and wealth are *not* the same thing. Wealth is highly personal. Wealth could mean you have your health, a good family life, a car that runs, and you live modestly. To someone else, wealth could mean luxury cars and a big house. Wealth has nothing to do with the amount of money you have; it's more your personal definition. So it makes sense that in order to build wealth, we must first define what wealth means to you.

I encourage you to take a few minutes to write down your definition of wealth. Go deep. Use all your senses. Write about wealth like you have it now. Writing in present tense in positive terms is part of working on your mind-set. If you were wealthy according to your values, where would you be living? Who would be there with you? What are you wearing? What are you eating? What do your surroundings look like? What would you be doing with your free time? What passions would your wealth allow you to pursue? Where would you go for your perfect vacation? Who would you give or contribute to? You get the idea—now write.

In order to build wealth on your terms, you must first begin by finding out how much income you want to build that will allow you to live the way you want to live. This means you're going to have to sit down with a pencil or pen and some paper and do some number crunching. Don't let this intimidate you. How can you achieve your goal of wealth if you don't know what your target is? Knowing your numbers is crucial. It will be the target you need to guide you to take those daily baby steps.

Have you ever made a New Year's resolution, only to abandon it by February? Many people do. In fact, according to *Inc.* magazine, 60 percent of people abandon their resolutions within six months.[1] Know why? Because they didn't take the time to visualize, get specific, and write their goals down.

The good news is that you can start to get serious about goal setting right here, right now. That's why I wrote this book! Studies show that you are 42 percent more likely to achieve your goals if you write them down. That's why I am asking you to spend some time defining and writing down

[1] Peter Economy, "This Is the Way You Need to Write Down Your Goals for Faster Success," Inc., https://www.inc.com/peter-economy/this-is-way-you-need-to-write-down-your-goals-for-faster-success.html.

exactly what wealth looks like for you. I am also going to ask you to come up with a number that represents the amount of income you are going to need to live off your real estate investments alone. Can you believe that's possible? Living off your real estate investments?

The good news is that you can start to get serious about goal setting right here, right now.

To discover that number, you will need to know what your monthly debts are, as opposed to your monthly income. I have done this process, and I know you can do it too. Remember, baby steps. Review your bank statements for the past six months, then itemize and calculate what you've been spending on gas, rent, mortgage, cell phone bills, car payments, credit card debt, children's expenses, student loans, insurance, cable, electricity, food, shopping, shoes, purses, clothes, make-up, restaurants, grocery stores, movies, even those monthly subscriptions like Amazon Prime and Netflix or Spotify. Write everything down month by month. There are plenty of great budgeting apps or worksheets that you can find on the internet. If it helps, use one of those. You don't need to, but it might help you organize your thoughts if the process feels overwhelming. It's important to take the time to be as accurate as you can about this. Remember, it's moving you toward your financial freedom.

After you have your monthly expenses and income calculated for six months, you'll need to figure out your average spending by adding up all your expenses for that six months period and dividing it by six. The reason we average your expenses over six months like this is because we all buy extra things now and then or have expenses that don't reoccur from month to month (like car or home repairs).

Let's imagine, for example, your monthly average expense is $5,000. Let's pad this amount by 15 percent ($750), just to be safe for those extra things we forget about. Let's round up your number to $6,000 so we have a whole number for the sake of this example.

Now that you know you need $6,000 per month to live comfortably, you have a goal to aim for. You won't get there all at once. It's just like setting a New Year's resolution to lose twenty pounds. You don't lose the weight all in one week. It's healthier for you to lose it slowly. The same is true here.

I call the final number you came up with your "freedom number." In this case, $6,000 is the freedom number or the foundation for building wealth. Without determining an end number, how would you know where to begin?

Wealth building in real estate investing begins with one property at a time. We often hear people talk about real estate investing in big numbers—people, for example, who own huge apartment complexes with hundreds of units. And maybe that's why this business is so intimidating to many women. Those huge numbers can be overwhelming.

Remember my friend Holly from New York? Her numbers are huge, but she didn't start out that way. Most people can't even imagine themselves dealing with numbers like that. But they can imagine one small step at a time. So that's where we start. I want you to challenge your comfort zone, but not throw yourself into overwhelmed mode, because that's a surefire way to fail. If you are to be successful at this, you must take measured action and assign yourself written goals.

Every successful investor has a story of starting small. I found it helpful and still do, talking to investors and asking questions relating to their successes. It may be helpful for you to ask people who are doing well on how they got started. Investors love to share their stories.

I would like to share mine.

After nine years of working in the lending industry, I bought my first home in 1999. It was a feat I never thought I could accomplish. The concept was there, I was in the heart of the industry that gives loan approvals to people and knew exactly what it took for them to get approved, but I never connected it with my possibility, my reality. Until that one day, when I decided to conquer my limiting beliefs regarding my income and decided to get preapproved.

I took the initiative to complete an application and gather my documents. In knowing exactly what the lender required, within a day or so, the loan officer gave me the exciting news and said I was preapproved for an FHA loan. They issued a preapproval letter, and off I went to shop for my very first place. It was exciting. I purchased a two-bedroom, one-and-a-half bathroom condo for about $105,000. Today those condos are selling north of $350,000, around the same price, if not better, as they were back in 2005 when the market was at its peak!

After a couple of years of living there, I decided to purchase a bigger place. My condo had risen to a value of $175,000 by then, so I took the equity and used it as a down payment for my next place, which was a three-bedroom, two-and-a-half bath townhouse in a much better area.

I bought that home for $330,000 in 2001. By 2006, my townhouse had risen to a value of $600,000. I knew that because there was a similar unit that sold in the same complex. It almost doubled in value after only five years, and that meant my equity had almost doubled too.

I was extremely proud of this accomplishment. It never crossed my mind that if I had helped my siblings buy a

If you are to be successful at this, you must take measured action and assign yourself written goals.

property and financed their homes in my name, I would be in trouble one day. I was so excited to help them that off I went, shopping with them and putting their mortgage in my name because I was certain they would have no problem paying it monthly, and I trusted their sense of responsibility. But the tide was about to turn. Because I was not the only decision maker in my household, when I mentioned we should sell and rent for a little while as I had been hearing a lot of a market shift, my other half said no. So I listened and we stayed. Never mind what was about to happen with my sibling's properties.

This point is important to mention because other people can alter or deflect your decisions even if your reasons are justifiable and noteworthy. Or even if your gut tells you so. I recall this decision vividly because it taught me a great life lesson.

We stayed, and by December 2007, we felt the real estate market and the lending industry start to crumble unlike anything we had ever felt. By 2008, the subprime lenders were imploding, causing a ripple effect to other lenders which quickly spread to other institutions. Hundreds of thousands of people were getting laid off, my sisters and I among them. The media cataloged the catastrophic financial crisis as it unfolded daily on the news of which companies and industries were crashing: Lehman Brothers, World Savings, New Century, Washington Mutual, and AIG to name a few companies never to be seen again.

Needless to say, for a few years it was a sad and depressing time, one that came to be known as the Great Recession. We were in the middle of the recession storm.

Not only was this felt nationwide but also worldwide. Many people in their respective countries were shown day after day in great despair and agony. The depression was felt everywhere. Work was unsteady, many were unemployed, and their income was slashed. To add salt to my personal wounds, my mom passed away in 2009. I was probably at my lowest point in my life during this time. Life was hard, and I was depressed. I did not know what to do or where to go. It was awful.

The well-illustrated diagrams that follow came courtesy of my financial advisor, Peter Mallouk, to illustrate what an economic recession looks like and how the economy bounces back. As I write, we are facing yet another economic crisis caused by a virus identified as SARS-CoV-2 (aka, COVID-19). Many call this one of the worst disease outbreaks the world has ever seen.

We are facing unprecedented times. As of yet, and as much money as there is floating out there, scientists have no cure for COVID-19—nor are they even close to one. The best defense to date is social distancing, and self-care.

Navigating a Pandemic: The Shape of the Recovery

One can't watch or read any daily news without seeing a new perspective on the "shape of the recovery," with economists, money managers, and pundits strongly arguing their respective points. In this letter, we will outline the more popular theories. Get ready for some alphabet soup!

A "V-Shaped Recovery" takes place when the economy rapidly contracts into recession and is then followed by a sharp, strong recovery. A graph of an economic recovery in this fashion resembles the shape of a "V."

Most economic recoveries resemble this shape, as historically, the harder the fall, the stronger and swifter the recovery. This is especially true when the cause of the economic shock is external, as is the case here. If not for the coronavirus, most think we would still be in the middle of the longest bull market in history. The tech bubble recovery was a V-shaped recovery that was short lived, as it was quickly followed by 9/11. A V-shaped recovery means everyone quickly gets back to business and spending. The International Monetary Fund currently predicts a V-shaped recovery, as does every other pundit on TV.

A "U-Shaped Recovery' is when things recover in a healthy fashion, and relatively quickly, but by no means is it "all systems go." In other words, people get back to business, but in a more gradual fashion.

Under this scenario, things are getting better all the time, and there are no major setbacks, but it takes months or even a year or more to get to full steam again.

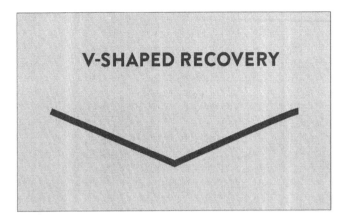

Our most recent recovery, after the 2008/2009 financial crisis, was a U-shaped recovery, albeit a far slower one than normal. By comparison, if we are really in a U-shaped recovery now, we are on pace to recover several years faster than we did after 2008/2009. Those predicting a U-shaped recovery include JP Morgan, ING, and CNBC's Jim Cramer. A U-shaped recovery is also the favorite choice of 50 economists surveyed by Reuters.

A "W-Shaped Recovery" takes place when the economy rapidly contracts, appears to sharply recover, only to collapse again before the real recovery. A graph of an economic recovery in this fashion resembles the shape of a "W." The early 1980s recession, one some readers may recall, is the most recent example of a W-shaped recovery. In 1980, the economy fell into recession, only to quickly recover. The recovery took place so quickly that high inflation accompanied it. The Fed dramatically raised interest rates to slow inflation, only to drive the economy back into recession. The economy ultimately

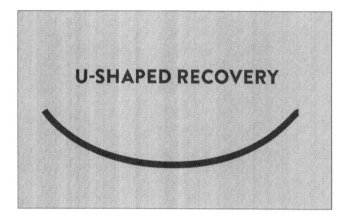

recovered in 1983 and continued a period of incredible growth that went on for over fifteen years.

Many economists believe we are in the middle of a classic W-shaped recession. They hold that the V-shaped recovery we are currently experiencing is really the middle of a W-shaped recovery, which means we are in for another massive move downward before the real recovery begins.

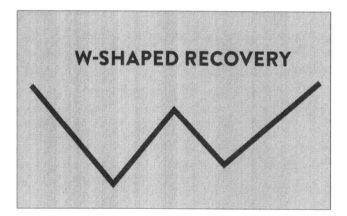

This group of prognosticators, which includes Moody's Analytics, argues that the recent stock market run-up is really a head fake.

With an "L-Shaped Recovery," the economy stays weak for many years until it finally recovers. An L-shaped recovery has never happened in the United States. For a modern-day example, we need to look to Japan, which plummeted into a severe recession in the late 1980s, taking nearly twenty years to recover, and never again reaching its rapid growth rates. In short, this would be really, really bad. Barclay's says there is a "chance" of an L-shaped recovery. Of course, there is a chance for anything to happen.

Many economists believe we are in the middle of a classic W-shaped recession.

Quickly running out of letters, we turn to a mathematical symbol, the square root. With a "Square Root Recovery," the economy plummets, quickly recovers, then stays flat for a period of years. The idea of a "square root" recovery is new, and there are no modern historical examples of it, but, hey, there's a first for everything.

We could go on and on here. There's talk of a "Nike swoosh" recovery, which implies we have seen the bottom already and will embark on a slow upward trajectory. And heck, you can make up any shape you want. The only rule is

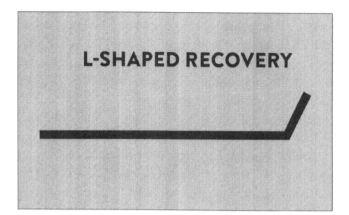

the line needs to keep moving to the right. If you can make a shape that follows the left to right rule, well, it can happen.

So What Is One to Do with All This?

An investor who believes in a V-shaped recovery would likely do best entirely invested in stocks, as a recovery can only be sustained if corporate profits increase, thus driving up stock prices. Someone with very high conviction would load up on small cap stocks, with the knowledge that in nine of the ten most recent recessions, they have greatly outperformed on the upslope. An investor believing in a U-shaped recovery would also invest heavily in stocks and tilt to smaller stocks, knowing that the market moves ahead of the economy. An investor believing in a W-shaped recovery would rotate from bonds to stocks, then back to bonds, and finally again to stocks during each step of the recovery (good luck with that). An investor believing we are in the midst of an L-shaped or square root recovery would be best served in bonds, as the

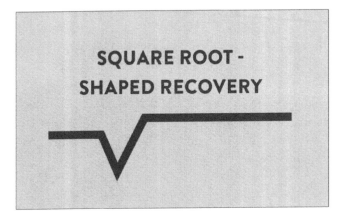

yield received would be one of the best investments available in an economy weak enough that companies aren't profitable and real estate prices stay low due to lack of demand.

. . . .

Along with every defeat, whether you're getting knocked out in the ring, missing that touchdown by mere inches, or failing to finish the race, there's always that story of how a person rose up from the rubble, rose up from the failure. It is part of our lessons in life: We fail, then we succeed, then fail again and then again succeed. It is the circle of life in which we live and that which keeps us going. Staying complacent is not where we're meant to be. I did not like being in that state, so I changed it.

During the worst times in real estate (and in my life) was when I entered in as a real estate broker. I pulled myself out of that rubble, dusted off the despair, and got over the sadness and the loss to begin focusing on helping people with their real estate investments and short sale transactions. I also worked with banks on their REOs (real estate owned). Helping others gave me the reason to get up and live on. There were lots of people who needed help, plenty of homeowners who wanted out of their homes and out of their high-balance mortgages. They wanted to walk away from their upside-down home and mortgage payments and start a new life.

It was an easy transition for me because I knew how to maneuver them through the short-sale process from years of experience in the lending industry. I even helped homeowners stay in their homes by assisting with their loan modification, I myself had to do a loan modification then a short sale soon after.

When I began to notice the real estate market moving upward, I decided to purchase my first investment property. It was a two-bedroom, one-bath condo in Antioch that I bought toward the end of 2011 for $30,000. I wasn't sure whether to rent it or sell after it was fixed up. Because the area wasn't that safe and I began seeing a positive movement in the real estate market in 2012, I decided to sell after owning it for about five months for $55,000. A great return of $5,000 a month. I reinvested the $25,000 equity to purchase a rental property by doing a 1031 exchange. I then purchased a two-bedroom, two-bathroom condo for $60,000 in a better location in the same city and rented it.

A 1031 exchange is an excellent way of diverting taxes from the IRS by exchanging it for a like-kind property. In this example, I purchased a condo for a condo, but you can 1031 into just about any transaction, as long as it's considered real estate.

My relatives, who were buying very inexpensive properties out of state with excellent cash-flow through a network group, began telling me with excitement about what they were doing and how successful they've been. I couldn't help but to take action and try it as well. After almost three years of being a landlord in California, I decided to sell that condo, which sold for $120,000, by doing another 1031 exchange. This time, I was able to purchase four properties. One I purchased in cash; as for the other three, I divided the remaining funds to use as down payment and financed

> *Staying complacent is not where we're meant to be. I did not like being in that state, so I changed it.*

the rest, using leverage. From when I began, on that pivotal month of January 2015, I have not stopped.

Currently, I own thirteen "doors" including my primary, and I'm in contract to purchase a new construction duplex in North Texas and another duplex in Ohio. I have a goal to purchase a certain number of properties each year because at the end of the fourth year, I will have fifty doors that are all cash flowing. I started with a number as illustrated in an earlier chapter, then came up with the total number of doors I would need in order to achieve that number.

Like some of you, I started with nothing but a thought, an idea, and with some fear and trepidation, I decided to take a leap of faith and began with baby steps, and here I am five years later still working on my plans and goals. I never forget that goal in front of me. It's a journey, a process, an everyday action of drinking water before I get out of bed, being grateful for waking up alive and healthy.

Now, it's not a walk in the park owning these properties, nor is it all rainbows and unicorns, but it is an asset that's tangible versus the stock market, and it doesn't fluctuate like the stock market. Technically, my mortgage is paid by my tenants from my rental properties, so my ROI (return on investment) more than pays for itself. Each property cash-flows. Some of them will be in areas where they will also grow in equity. It's been one of the best decisions I have made since being at the lowest point of my life. I could not be more grateful and humbled.

Most successful female investors started out just like me, a little bit nervous and unsure. Perhaps this is how you are feeling too. It's okay, though, because this is normal. We are all scared of making the wrong choice, but we all have one thing in common: a better financial future, the opportunity to build wealth, and the ability to enjoy freedom according to our own terms. I was seeking this kind of lifestyle. I just didn't know it until I took action.

If you have children, think about the gift you can give them by teaching them these simple methods to manage their own wealth. These actionable steps are not taught in school. You will also be modeling an entrepreneurial spirit for them. You will be showing them that the conventional model of going to school, getting a degree, and working at a job you may or may not like for the next forty years isn't the only way to live. You will be teaching your children to look for opportunities where others only see problems. You will be demonstrating creativity and empowering behavior. Truly, this can change the trajectory of lives.

Isn't it time you started? What kind of property are you thinking of purchasing today? How much is it? What does leveraging look like for *you*?

Each property cash-flows. Some of them will be in areas where they will also grow in equity.

_____

_____

_____

_____

_____

_____

_____

_____

_____

_____

_____

_____

_____

_____

_____

_____

_____

_____

_____

_____

_____

_____

_____

_____

_____

_____

_____

_____

_____

_____

_____

_____

_____

_____

_____

_____

_____

_____

_____

_____

_____

_____

_____

_____

_____

_____

_____

_____

_____

_____

_____

_____

_____

_____

_____

_____

_____

_____

Adopt the Habits of Successful Investors

You have to practice success. Success doesn't just show up.
If you aren't practicing success today, you won't wake up
in 20 years and be successful, because you won't have
developed that habits of success, which are small things
like finishing what you start, putting a lot of effort into
everything you do, being on time, treating people well.

Michelle Obama

We all have habits. These are the behaviors we do over and over without even thinking. There are good habits, like brushing your teeth before you go to bed, and not-so-good habits, like overindulging in sugar. We are all a mixture of both kinds. I like the above quote by our former first lady Michelle Obama because it really gets to the heart of how important mind-set and habits are in determining the trajectory you choose to set for your financial future. It all starts with the mind-set, and then it becomes a reality when you put your mind, heart, and soul into it. Oh, and a lot of practice and effort too.

According to an article in *Inc.* magazine, successful businesspeople share some common characteristics when it comes to habits. I won't share them all here, but I will highlight the ones that are most applicable to success in real estate investing.

1. Read everything you can about the industry. Most successful real estate investors spend a designated amount of time every day reading about the trends in their market. If you are a beginner, you may not remember it all, but I guarantee your brain will store the information for you, and one day it will suddenly make sense. Find a time to read (or listen to audiobooks or podcasts) each day. Add it to your calendar as a repeating date with yourself. Look at the Bigger Pockets or Real Wealth Network websites for inspiration and reading resources.

2. Keep a journal. Guess what? Not only are you more likely to achieve goals that you write down, but science has shown us that when we write things down, they are more likely to "stick" in our brains. It's those seeds you plant that will take root to achieving your goal and one day being able to harvest what you've sown.

3. Surround yourself with positive people. Have you ever heard that saying about how you become like the five people with whom you spend the most time? It's true. So why hang around with naysayers and negative people?

Spend time with people who are living the way you want to live. These are the people who will challenge you to become a little bit better every day. They don't have to be other women real estate investors (but if you can find them, they are good to have in your corner). Just try to make an effort to be around positive, successful people. Everyone's definition of success will be different, so choose according to your definition. Feed your mind with positivity.

4. Pick three things you must accomplish every day. Are you one of those people with an endless to-do list? Many women are. That can be demoralizing because you'll never complete a to-do list like that! It will only set you up for failure and feeling bad about yourself at the end of each day. Why not pick three things from your list (preferably, things that expand your comfort zone) and make them priorities each day? Ask yourself the WIN question: What's Important Now? These are the things that must get done if you are to advance yourself in your real estate investing goals. They are nonnegotiable. Then do them. Take action on something that advances your real estate investing goals every day. Hold yourself accountable for these actions. This will make you feel successful because you already know that your beliefs are your reality.

5. Develop a positive mind-set. I've left this one for last because it's my favorite. One of my daily habits is working on maintaining a positive mind-set. Just like you, I have bad days too. On those days I have to work a little harder on my mind-set. Mind-set is everything, and if you're in a state of worry or fear or negativity, it

will be impossible for you to achieve your dreams and goals or to even think positively. Remember that a dream or a goal is simply just an idea with a deadline. Anyone can dream, and anyone can set goals. It's only when you set a deadline and create action that it becomes reality. Developing a healthy habit around your mind-set will help you maintain your success on autopilot. If you don't have to think about the way you're going to go about your morning, for instance, you will have a habitual process that kicks your day off with success, Hal Elrod writes about this in his book *The Miracle Morning*.[1] Today, he talks to audiences around the world about how he

It's only when you set a deadline and create action that it becomes reality.

has a morning routine that kicks his day off for success, and the reason he has it is because he was given a second chance on life after a near-fatal car accident. Morning routines set the tone for the rest of your day. What is your morning routine? Or do you just get out of bed and wing it? How could you develop a new morning habit that would start the day off on a positive every day? What things would you do or say to yourself? Would you pray? Read? Write? Do yoga? Go to the gym? What feels good to you? It doesn't matter what you do as much as it matters that you do it every day until it becomes an act that you don't even think about anymore. That's what a habit is. Jot some ideas for your morning routine in the pages at the end of the chapter.

Resilience is a mind-set quality that is very important in real estate investing. What is resilience? It is the ability to turn the not-so-great things that happen in life into things that strengthen you. How resilient are you? What adversities have you faced in life that have helped you to grow and be stronger? Write them down. Then refer to them when you need a little extra help with your mind-set.

In terms of real estate, resilience will help you navigate through mistakes, volatility, and downturns. Don't let those things intimidate you. No one enjoys smooth sailing all the time, not in this business or any other, for that matter.

You've got to stay resilient and build success and wealth. People retire and live off the cash flow of their real estate investment properties. I've defined my financial freedom number, and my properties are cash flowing, but nothing is perfect. Tenants don't take care of properties, toilets break, and repairs cost money. You've got to be resilient. Just know that it's okay to fail—take the plunge and just dive in, even if it feels scary or uncertain.

My goal is to focus on cash flow over rehab. Whether it's rent or lease or Airbnb, my goal is to purchase a home that's ready and rent it. I've learned quite a bit about the real estate market since I first began. Now I'm focused on multi-unit properties and scaling up, but the core habits I maintain in my day-to-day life and my foundational principles are still the same.

Here are a few habits I've learned along the way for keeping my properties operating smoothly:

First, when you've got several properties, it's important to have an excellent property manager.

In Indianapolis, for instance, there is a strong market for equity and cash flow. I needed a property manager, so I found one. You've got to do your due diligence and connect with a property manager in a relational way. More importantly, you need to find one who is forthright each time you have to reach into your pocket. Trust that each work order, invoice, receipt, or document is accurate. In one of my properties, for example, there was a leak, with a $10,000 solution because they had to dig under the slab of a water heater. If I didn't have reliable property managers, I would have been pulling my hair out, dealing with details I'm not really suited for. You can't do everything if you want to grow.

In this particular case, the management company mismanaged that property, so I sold it and took those funds to purchase another through a 1031 exchange. In another situation in Michigan, a house was vacant for a month, and someone broke in and stole the copper pipes, putting a hole in the wall. Each one of these situations is a mental, emotional, and financial energy drainer. You've got to be prepared for adversity. Just know that it will make you more resilient over time. Remember this especially if you feel like screaming or crying. More importantly, remember that this is a business, *your* business, and sometimes problems arise in your businesses, but armed with the necessary resilience and knowledge, you will surely prevail.

A huge part of mind-set is your ability to develop personal relationships. The world truly revolves around relationships, and you can't sell anything without first engaging with someone else and creating a relationship where they learn that you have the knowledge and that they can trust you.

I am a real estate broker and have been helping clients for years, so I believe in this wholeheartedly. Connecting with people is one of the most important aspects to a smooth transaction or relationship. They have to know that you have their best interests at heart in order for them to do business with you.

How well are you building relationships today? A lot of it comes down to the value that you provide others. Provide value up front, and you'll be amazed how many people will begin to see your authenticity as something they're drawn to. People want to work with people they like and trust.

> *Connecting with people is one of the most important aspects to a smooth transaction or relationship.*

Be the one people want to work with. Some real estate agents get so hung up on the deal they forget about the relationship, and the next thing you know, the deal falls apart before it could even get started. Process is important, but people are even *more* important.

Mental management and good habits are crucial for success in this industry and in life. You must spend just as much time on personal growth as you do on learning about investing. Although it may initially seem like it has nothing to do with investing, it is everything. Start now. If you were to develop a power hour for yourself each morning, devoted to good habits of personal growth, what would it include? Do it and do it daily. Tweak it if necessary. The important thing is that you take action toward your wealth goals each and every day.

_____

_____

_____

_____

_____

_____

_____

_____

_____

_____

_____

_____

_____

_____

_____

_____

_____

_____

_____

_____

_____

_____

_____

_____

_____

_____

_____

_____

_____

_____

_____

_____

_____

_____

_____

_____

_____

_____

_____

_____

_____

_____

_____

_____

_____

_____

_____

_____

_____

_____

_____

_____

_____

_____

_____

_____

Start thinking about your ideal market. It can be whomever you want it to be. For me, it is women who have never invested in real estate or women who are investing but are stuck or want to achieve more.

Finding Investors

*Surround yourself only with people who are
going to take you higher.*

Oprah Winfrey

If you're not yet an investor but want to be, this section is for
you! Take it all in and learn as you go. If you're an investor
already, this section should help you think about how to find
more investors.

Where do you find your clients? If you're an investor in
real estate and want to expand, you may want to include a
coaching or seminar business as part of what you offer. Start
thinking about your ideal market. It can be whomever you
want it to be. For me, it is women who have never invested
in real estate or women who are investing but are stuck or
want to achieve more.

When I talk to others as a mentor or speak at a seminar,
one question always comes up: "How do I find investors?"

The best answer is to be proactive and establish a consistent niche. Make it authentic and unique.

Aligning with the right team or group—women wanting to invest in real estate who don't have their own real estate, license—is one way. You can always align yourself with home buyers as well. They need to find a trusted real estate agent as well as have relationships with mortgage brokers, title companies or attorneys, and a tax advisor. Treat your circle as a business and build an empire.

The same advice is true for anyone in any industry. Stay focused. Find your niche and focus on that one thing.

Partnering with others in business isn't unique to real estate investing. It's a practice as old as the mountains. There are many reasons you may want to partner with an investor. These are just a few:

1. Get the funds you need to acquire new properties.

2. Reduce your personal risk.

3. Do more deals.

4. Help other women succeed.

5. Spread your resources out.

6. Get better financing deals and gain more resources.

Real estate investing partnerships can appear in many different formats. As I mentioned in a previous chapter on leverage, they can be utilized as an investment partner to purchase larger deals like shopping malls, retail stores, or apartment buildings. For example, I joined two groups that were each purchasing properties for future building and needed funds in order to complete the projects.

This type of group is called a "syndication." A syndication is a group of individuals or organizations that combine to promote some common interest. With the two separate syndications I joined, one purchased an up-and-coming wine village and the other focused on new construction to build 200 houses in an up-and-coming community.

Crowdfunding and joint ventures are similar to syndications. Partnering with your parents is also an option, teaming up with folks with retirement money that is just sitting in a bank or 401k account earning 1 to 2 percent.

"How do I find investors?" The best answer is to be proactive and establish a consistent niche.

You can borrow these funds and offer to pay them a higher interest fee, like 5 or 6 percent, in return for them lending you the money for the investment.

For those who think they don't have any money or can't get the money to invest, there are ways. You just have to think outside the box and brainstorm resources. You can write a letter to people you know, about what your intentions are with their money. I know of investors who are successful with this method. I'm sure it's not an easy thing, asking to borrow people's money and having them trust that you'll take good care of it and, in return, give it back with interest. It's a simple process, but it's not easy to do because what you're asking is for people to part with their hard-earned savings so you can go and build a real estate portfolio with their funds. Obviously, there's a lot of trust that goes along with this. Once you are successful with taking on the practice of borrowing other people's money, you need to remember what a huge responsibility you've undertaken. Never take it lightly that people just want to lend you their money.

A syndication is a group of individuals or organizations that combine to promote some common interest.

Remember that relationship and trust (as we emphasized earlier) are keys to a successful outcome. Always keep this in mind, but also remember that life happens, and what you plan doesn't always come out the way it should. Investing is a risk, be it in real estate or the stock market.

There can be disadvantages to choosing investors, but if you do your due diligence, you can mitigate problems early on. Investors can change their minds even after they've signed on, partners become fearful and need to back out, or the deal doesn't come together. Worse yet, the property deal you were going to invest in with your investors collapses or falls apart. You are still left with those investor funds.

When you take other people's money and do it right, there are rules you have to follow. On a much bigger scale (as with syndications and crowdfunding), those people who take investors' money have to comply with SEC (Security and Exchange Commission) rules. Know the guidelines before taking other people's funds.

Ultimately, it's up to you to decide if you want to partner with investors. If you do, it can help propel you toward your goals on a much faster level than if you worked alone. It could make all the difference between achieving financial freedom next year or in ten years. Knowing this information, what kind of an investor are you? Would you invest with other people like your spouse, parents, or siblings, or would you rather go it alone?

_____

_____

_____

_____

_____

_____

_____

_____

_____

_____

_____

_____

_____

_____

_____

_____

_____

_____

_____

_____

_____

_____

_____

_____

_____

_____

_____

_____

_____

_____

_____

_____

_____

_____

_____

_____

Managing Your Self-Talk

*Kind words can be short and easy to speak,
but their echoes are truly endless.*

Mother Teresa

What is self-talk? What does it have to do with real estate investing?

Self-talk is talk or thoughts directed at yourself. Simply put, it means talking to yourself. It is something you do naturally throughout your waking hours. Self-talk is a powerful tool for increasing your self-confidence and curbing negative emotions.

Positive self-talk is the kind that is supportive and affirming and helps you cultivate positive thoughts and dispel the negative ones. It's the voice in your head that tells you "It's going to be okay and you are going to rise back up" when a setback occurs and derails your plans, or when your plans did not work out. It is a wonderful tool that we all already have in ourselves. And, it is free. Absolutely free!

So what does self-talk have to do with real estate investing?

Well, positive self-talk can be the foundation of your confidence in making a decision to invest. Not just investing in real estate but in any other kinds of investment with potential. Positive self-talk encourages you to take the chance, even though you are unsure and afraid of the negative consequences, the fear of failure in your decisions, the doubts that scream and echo in your mind, and the negative talk that goes round and round in your head. This rumination should be conquered by the positive self-talk so that you will not be bogged down by all the negative and pessimistic thoughts.

Self-talk is a powerful tool for increasing your self-confidence and curbing negative emotions.

These negative thoughts can grow and become self-defeating, which is not good at all in terms of investing—and in terms of everything else! Defeat the rumination and let the positive self-talk take over your mind. And then tell yourself to take that leap of faith and start investing! It is easier said than done, but you can *do* it!

I recently closed on a triplex in Alabama, which puts my real estate investment count at 13. And counting, I hope, God willing. I know what I want and I know what my goal is.

That is why focusing on the positive mind-set of abundance is so important to your building your business or your investments.

I know from experience that there's always going to be "noise" surrounding everything we do in life. When I set out to blaze a trail in writing my first book ever, there was a lot of noise in my head, hence the importance of self-talk. What you say to yourself matters. I was apprehensive at first and my mind kept asking my heart "Why do you want to do this?" or "Oh, what if people don't like it?"

There's always that hesitation and fear of the unknown. I think everybody feels that fear and uncertainty of going into something new or something they're unsure of. That's just being human, I think.

So how do you address that fear when you know that fear certainly is real? Well, the truth of the matter is, there will always be some kind of fear and uncertainty when it comes to putting your money into an investment. People also feel the same fear and hesitation when making almost any big decision, especially when there is money involved. And, to invest in whatever that it may be, is a big decision that one has to make.

When I first embarked upon my journey into the real estate investment realm, I had all the fears and doubts and hesitations there are out there. Because of all those risks involved in investing, I had already decided that I would not put all my money into the stock market. Yes, the profits can be quick and bountiful, but as quick as you can make them, you can lose them too. Because of this, I made a resolution to invest mostly in real estate. And the rest, as they say, is history.

Investing is, of course, a risky venture. All investments involve an element of risk. There are a lot of things to consider before you dive into it. The pros and cons have to be evaluated thoroughly before anything can happen. Yes, your investment could go belly up; yes, your investments could fail, but as much as there is a chance of failure, there is certainly a chance of success, right? You will never know unless you try.

With the elections coming up at the end of the 2020, there is a looming fear about how the elections will impact the real estate market. On top of that, with the ongoing COVID-19 pandemic, (as mentioned in a prior chapter) and its devastating impact on the world—socially, economically, financially, and in just about every other way imaginable—the

> # *The pros and cons have to be evaluated thoroughly before anything can happen.*

future is uncertain and appears to be bleak. This will definitely have an impact on the way we invest and connect, but this does not mean that there aren't investment opportunities out there. There are, especially in the real estate investment sector. The key is to invest strategically and smart in these difficult and precarious economic times.

One thing I know for sure is that we will always have economic troubles, whether it's a pandemic that changes the world and turns investments, the stock market, and banks upside down or something else. That's why I'm glad I invested in real estate. I keep thinking to myself, what if I had put all of my money on stocks? I find comfort in thinking of how I had listened to my instincts to invest in real estate and not all in stocks. Overall, my mind-set is that real estate investments are far more stable and solid than the other kinds of investments out there. They are also more consistent. Real estate is one of the most popular and profitable investments with a lot of potential for success if you do it right. Real estate investing offers many advantages, and investors can enjoy a steady financial income flow that will lead to financial freedom.

Here are some of the advantages of investing in real estate:

1. **Equity.** You can build equity as you whittle down your mortgage. As you build your equity, it gives you the leverage to invest in more rental properties and this will in turn increase your cash flow.

2. **Passive Income.** You can generate passive income that is almost tax free from your rental properties. Your rental properties will work for you no matter where you are, even while you are sleeping. The more rental properties you own, the more you'll be able to generate income that you can use to cover your expenses. And the more income you generate, the more freedom you will have to spend your time in leisure rather than work.

3. **Retirement Income Supplement.** When you invest in real estate strategically and smart, these investments can stably help you increase your wealth over time. The wealth that you accumulate can then provide cash flow and income supplement when you retire.

4. **Real Estate Value Appreciates Over Time.** Unlike assets such as cars, boats, computers, and furniture, real estate properties have a strong trend of appreciation, meaning that over time the value of the property increases. Why is that? Values increase for two reasons. The first is that rental rates will continue to rise because of the demand for these facilities and increasing construction costs. Second, with the number of investors bidding on real estate investments, the cap rate, or yield, will continue to compress, which increases values.

5. **Real Estate Investing Offers Flexibility.** When you invest in real estate, it gives you flexibility. The more properties you buy, the more portfolio you build over time. You can utilize your rental income to reinvest in another line of real estate like the fix-and-flip, wholesaling, or by investing in commercial properties. And this can be another viable source of your income. You can manage your properties around your own schedule or hire a property management company to do it to free up your "work" time to "me" time. This flexibility of setting your own schedule is quite wonderful. In addition, investing in real estate does not have a salary cap, so your earning potential can be limitless.

Do you think managing your self-talk is important to investing? How would you manage your self-talk? What would you say to eliminate the noise inside? Write your ideas down.

_____

_____

_____

_____

_____

_____

_____

_____

_____

_____

_____

_____

_____

_____

_____

_____

_____

_____

_____

_____

_____

_____

_____

_____

_____

_____

_____

_____

_____

_____

_____

_____

_____

_____

_____

_____

_____

_____

_____

_____

_____

_____

*A saying and a word,
a leap of faith and
authenticity, are going to
be those powerful words
you see and read to remind
yourself of what you can do
and who you are.*

A Leap of Faith with Authenticity

Refuse to be that person that, like so many others, is still driving down the same road, years down the line, mournfully longing to go back in time to be given just one more chance to take the road that they know they should have taken because they dismissed all possible, extraordinary signs. It'll never get easier to make the leap and this is your chance; so make the change. Take the road now.

Victoria Erickson

Authenticity is something we have or don't have. It's a practice—a conscious choice of how we want to live. Authenticity is a collection of choices that we have to make every day. It's about the choice to show up and be real. The choice to be honest. The choice to let our true selves be seen.

Brené Brown

A saying and a word, a leap of faith and authenticity, are going to be those powerful words you see and read to remind yourself of what you can do and who you are. Say it out loud and let it sink into your mind and heart until it gives you the energy you need to take action. Taking that leap of faith is how I began my journey in baby steps into the unknown with no experience. Reading and listening to others who have done what you're about to do is one thing, but to actually doing it takes a leap of faith. The unknown we associate with faith is either spiritual or believing in something higher than yourself.

I didn't know what I was getting into in 2012. The only memory I had was the huge wound that left me scarred from the credit crisis in 2008. That rang true again when I decided to lift myself and begin again in real estate investing. No doubt it was there, but something else was gnawing at me, an even bigger desire to grow and to not let fear keep me down.

Although I loved helping people with their short sales and loan modifications and banks with their REOs, I felt I was leaving myself behind. I helped buyers purchase and negotiate the best deals for them. I helped investors scale up in their business. I was playing a key role in helping my clients increase their portfolio, which was great, but I also had the desire to do what they were doing.

Our brain keeps in it millions of memories, and on this particular day, because it has the tendency to keep us safe, the archive brought forward the painful memory of what happened the last time I owned several properties. But having experienced a hurtful past and seeing the economy move forward and grow, I was driven to overcome that memory, to be a part of the movement that was happening in real estate and move ahead despite what could happen. In fact, I knew it was going to be more painful to stay in my comfort zone than to take that leap of faith and try again. I refused to stay where I was, in fear-based thinking. I could not do that to myself regardless of what happened in the past.

From 2012 on, I have not stopped. This, I know, you can overcome too. The constant reminder of it will be more painful to stay in your comfort than to grow should be what keeps you going.

I knew it was going to be more painful to stay in my comfort zone than to take that leap of faith and try again.

By now, you've written goals down, perhaps even visualized what your first property will look like, how your process will begin and how your tenants will be paying your mortgage payment. Why not take these two powerful words and take action? What would it look like if you took a leap of faith?

Take this book for example. I had lots of fear from the outset, so it took a while for me to get started. In the middle of writing the book, I had paused a lot and for quite some time too. Even now, nearing the end, I still find myself pausing, here and there, and for some periods of time. It's taken over two years to complete. As you can see from an idea where the seed first germinated in my mind, I fueled it with desire and kept it burning. This is probably one of my longest commitments besides the 23-year relationship I've shared with my partner.

Authenticity can be a challenge if you're not aware of your own capabilities or purpose in life. When you know what you're good at, do that. Discovering your purpose is essential to your authenticity.

How can you make the daily choice to live your truth each day? Be intentional. Take time to be intentional about your purpose. Follow your purpose and remain confident in yourself. Even if you don't know how to do something, just keep pushing forward! By learning, you are essentially practicing your baby steps. Success takes time, and it often comes with challenges and frustrations. No matter who you are, frustration and emotion are part of the entrepreneurial process. The skills you develop over time will add to your authenticity.

I've had some interesting experiences over the years. For example, because of the lack of inventory in real estate throughout the San Francisco Bay Area, a house can sell way over asking price. A house in San Francisco can get an offer half a million dollars over its asking price. This leads people to wonder if the price was real or genuine to begin with.

It's crazy but it's true. We have lived in a seller's market for over a decade, and demand is sometimes through the roof. The supply deficiency of real estate properties will always cause the prices to shoot up, and as our population increases, the demand for homes will definitely surpass supply. This will be advantageous for real estate investors. Unfortunately, this often leads to egregious behavior by those acting out of greed, an obvious detriment to those who play ethically.

No matter how our economy is doing, there will always be investors looking for those golden opportunities available out there. They will buy and sell real estate every day, regardless of how the economy is doing, because at the end of the day, everybody needs a place to call home. Someone who needs a home will want to buy, someone who needs or wants to upgrade to a bigger home will be on the hunt, or a real estate investor will want to add to their portfolio.

What you need to know as an investor is where to look for these markets. If you're going to invest, you have to do thorough market research and find out which states, which

> *Discovering your purpose is essential to your authenticity.*

counties, and which cities are best for you. You want to look at the rental markets and see what best suits you, your capital, and your interests. Do your due diligence and research, especially if you're doing this long term. The good news is, all this research can be done from the comfort of your own home, online. The internet has made our lives so much easier today, I couldn't imagine not having the ability to access it.

In wearing two hats, as a real estate broker and real estate investor, I'm directly involved in all the issues my clients are in. Remember that as an investor, the emotions and the processes are different from each other because you're directly involved in all the issues your clients are in. I often run into similar situations with one property or another. What's important to know is there isn't going to be that perfect property where no issues crop up, especially if you have more than two. Even if you have just one, let's say the home you live in runs into problems such as a broken pipe or a leaky toilet or roof. The goal is to not let this get you down. Focus on the bigger picture, your goals, and what your certainty of purpose is. Build on those and you will be able to handle the adversities when they come. And always remember the saying "This too shall pass."

Self-care and self-enhancement are very important for me to practice on a daily basis because if I feel great on the inside, I am a better person on the outside along with being able to be the awesome realtor and investor I am meant to be. I connect with others more effectively and am able to build stronger, more solid relationships. I communicate with authenticity. I face challenges and adversities with solutions.

What does authenticity mean to you? How do you describe being authentic with someone? Are you being true to yourself and taking great care of your mind and body? What practices or habits could you do on a daily basis? Write down your answer.

· · · ·

In the beginning, I asked you what your dream was, and in each chapter I asked you a couple more questions. I wanted to make this book interactive by providing blank pages for you to write in after each chapter and to jot down your thoughts. I hope it was simple to follow, and even if you're not the type to write things down, I hope at least I got you started with that. These words you've written will be your recipe, your own thoughts and ideas. Remember they can be changed much like ingredients in your dishes; sometimes it just tastes *better* with an added ingredient or condiment. Your real estate investing journey will be much the same until you find the system that works for you. The ideas you've written down is the beginning, and my hope is that you follow it up by taking action, because this is where the magic happens.

I wrote this book because I am passionate about investing in real estate and noticed the lack of women investors throughout the world and wanted to share with as many of them as possible. If I was able to educate, provide to any woman through this book, the drive, that itself is awe-inspiring. I am deeply honored if I was able to strike inspiration and pique interest and to have reached you in a way that helps you learn to live financially free, to have financial abundance, to give more, to leave a future for your children, and to have the freedom to do whatever it is you want. Because you deserve it.

We can do this ladies, and we can do it together. We can do it in baby steps or take leaps forward. So do not wait. Start where you are standing and begin at once. In the meantime, I'll leave you with a quote from a woman who inspires me along with millions of others.

Our deepest fear is not that we are insignificant, our deepest fear is that we are powerful beyond measure.

Marianne Williamson

A Leap of Faith with Authenticity

_____

_____

_____

_____

_____

_____

_____

_____

_____

_____

_____

_____

_____

_____

_____

_____

_____

_____

_____

_____

_____

_____

_____

_____

_____

_____

_____

_____

_____

_____

_____

_____

_____

_____

_____

_____

_____

_____

Acknowledgments and Dedications

First and foremost, I'd like to thank God. For You have given me the light, the spirit and strength to be all that I can be. Each day I am alive and well is because of You! To the couple who gave me life, I'd like to thank my mom and dad, Dominador and Jane Cacanindin. Even though both of you are no longer here, I'm reminded every second of the impact you have made in my life . . . from bringing me into this world then to America and instilling in me the values of resiliency to keep going no matter how hard things get. We sure had our special moments. My dad used to say, "You can do it!" Simple words with immense impact. I never stop thinking of you, Dad. I wish you and Mom were here to help me see this book through, but I know you're smiling big from heaven.

My partner of 23 years, Noraya Mohd Yusuf. I also refer to you as my grammar queen. Thank you for the commitment in our relationship and your touches to the words in the book. You are a true example of pushing forward even when times get hard. I love you!

My sisters and their significant others, Jeana and Chris; the-wonderful-G-twin-powers, Gaye and Ronnie, Gail and Tom, Irish and Peter, Irene and AJ and Jazmine and Marquez. I come from a family of strong women. Thank you for inspiring me to keep going. A special thank you to Jeana for helping with editing. I am grateful for all of you and the closeness and bond we have with each other. Thanks to our parents for playing a key role in family values.

To my nieces and nephews: Arianna, Leila, Lilliana, Dominic, and Jeremiah. I am a better person because of you. My hope is for each and every one of you to be amazing individuals and great contributors to your family and community. I dedicate this book to you and hope you will read it and follow the steps and create a life of abundance for yourselves. I love you to the moon and back.

I'd also like to make a special dedication to my niece, Lilliana Isabel Arroyo, who was born into this world almost seven years ago with a large bladder, small colon, and intestines that have low to no movement. The organs are there, they just don't function like they should. Let that sink in for a minute, she's missing four vital organs, yet by the grace of God, she is alive and thriving. This super rare disease called Berdon Syndrome or MMIH Megacystis (means enlarged bladder), Microcolon (means small colon), Intestinal Hypoperistalsis (means low to no motility in her intestines) currently has no cure, but I have faith that one day, with all the technology and modern science out there one will be found very soon. Lilli is my "superhero" and is the reason for the many goals I strive to accomplish. You are the fuel to my energy. You inspire and drive me to stay on course and remain focused and persistent. My wish for you, Lilli, is for you to do the basic simple things that majority of us get to do, like eat and go to the bathroom. You are the epitome of full-of-life and zest. You are also super funny and witty. I am so grateful to be your auntie. I love watching you grow and become stronger and smarter. You also have a story to tell and I hope to be there when you scribe it through the pages of your book to share with the world. I love you with every pulse of my beating heart and pray you outlive me.

To my half-brother, Thomas Mendoza; his wife, Mona; and their beautiful girls and my nieces, Clarissa and Alyza who live in the Philippines. We may not see very much of you, but I'm grateful for Facebook because of the connection it gives me with you. I think of you often and dedicate this book to you and our family there.

To my closest relatives, our "ride-or-die" family, Gerald (Bong) and his wife, Janet; and their handsome sons, Andrew and Anthony. Can't forget their other four-legged loved ones, Sol and Luna. Grace (Apple) and her husband Al; their beautiful children, Kailea, Kyreece, Kamiya, and Khalil (my godson); and grandchildren, Isaiah and Kamaya. Gwen (Peaches) and her husband, Eric; and their four-legged kids, Smokey and Skye. Glenda (Cherry) and her boyfriend, JP. Angelo (Bam Bam). My awesome auntie and uncle who gave birth to them, Angel (Boogie) and Vicky (Olga) Agustin. Thank you for being like parents to me and my sisters. I dedicate this book to you all as each of you have played an important role in my life. I am so thankful for each of you and the closeness we have developed and continue to nurture over the years. I love you!

To the child I was fostering, whom we call Isa. My intentions were to adopt him, but it is not within God's plan this time around. You have brought an unbelievable amount of joy into my life and I'm humbled by the experience of unconditional love with you. I look forward to continuing to be a part of your life and seeing you evolve and become an amazing person.

To all my aunts and uncles still alive today, Auntie Veron, Auntie Evelyn, Uncle Rudy, Auntie Ida, and Auntie Chit. Even though we don't see each other, there is a part of you in this book through the spiritual connection of my parents' love.

To my closest friends, Audrey Muller and her wife, Samantha Thrower, Susie Garcia, Tina Paclebar, and Jane Nacelli, with their daughter and my goddaughter Kameron, Bee Sevikul, and Felicia DeMita, with their daughter

Noelle, Jenn Lee, Renee Cunningham, Estie Briggs-Whiteman, April Natividad, and Sheryl Uyan. Thanks to each and every one of you for the support and friendship you've given me throughout the years. We've shared lots of great memories and I will forever embrace them. I look forward to many more. Thank you for being a part of my life and showering it with joy and love.

To my relatives Craig and Arlene Turner along with their beautiful intelligent kids, Donny, Rachel, Robbie, and Tommy. Thank you for the love and connection and for the introduction to Real Wealth Network. From that introduction to years of investing is the culmination of this book. I am forever grateful.

To Kathy and Rich Fettke, the owners of Real Wealth Network. Thank you for having a place for people to go to. I'm grateful for being on your show, podcast #714, sharing my experience from housing crisis losses to success with single-family rentals.

I would like to also thank OnFire Books, Tammy Kling, and her team of women experts for helping with editing and the idea of making this book interactive. Thank you to my publisher, Larry Carpenter at Clovercroft Publishing and his team of experts for weaving the pages smoothly together. Thank you to Debbie Manning Sheppard for the great idea of my book cover, it's eye-catchy and inspiring.

To future investors, women or men, new or experienced, my hope is that by some grace of words in these pages you are inspired to take action in investing in yourself by investing in real estate. I have created a website www.thepowerofrealestateinvestingforwomen.com where you are free to share your views, experiences, or comments. I can also be reached through my Facebook business page Plenty of Realty.